Short ish walks
near the
Land's End

Paul White

Bossiney Books · Launceston

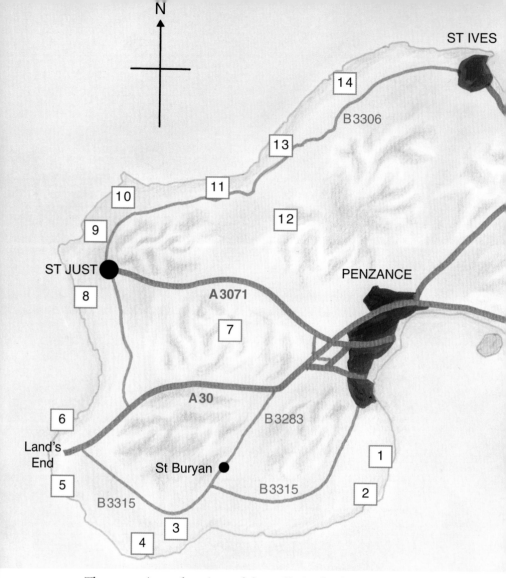

The approximate locations of the walks in this book

Introduction

A 'shortish' walk is typically 6-8 km (4-5 miles) in length, and likely to take 2-3 hours. How long you actually take will depend on your fitness, the weather conditions, and how much you find to interest you along the way. All the walks are circular, often involving a stretch of cliff path and an inland return. There are two wholly inland walks.

You will find that the Land's End peninsula ('West Penwith') is a totally fascinating landscape, quite unlike anywhere else, even within Cornwall. It is distinct in its geology, for this is where the granite meets the sea, with the most remarkable scenic effects: this also accounts for the remains of a mining industry more than 2000 years old – the ancient Greeks referred to it – because tin and copper are found near the rim of the granite outcrops. On a first visit, the juxtaposition of glorious scenery and derelict mining sites may seem incongruous, but it lies at the heart of Cornwall's sense of identity.

The walks may be shortish, but most of them are tough going in places, especially on the cliff path. You will find strenuous ascents and descents and some very uneven walking, as well as innumerable stiles due to the small fields which are so characteristic of the area. Proper walking boots are vital for grip and ankle support and a walking pole or stick is useful for balance in the descents. On the inland sections you may well find muddy patches even in dry weather, not to mention briars, thistles, gorse and nettles, so bare legs are a liability.

Safety – a real issue for walkers in this area

Cliff walking can be very exposed: the wind-chill factor is like being out in the Atlantic, and of course Cornish weather can change very rapidly, so you need extra layers of clothing, as well as waterproofs, for what is often an abrupt change of temperature between inland and cliff walking.

The most obvious hazard is the cliff path. It is not fenced off from the drop and in some of the walks passes alarmingly near the edge – see comments on individual walks if you suffer from vertigo. Walk no nearer the drop than you have to and keep a close eye on children and dogs. It is not safe to walk the cliffs in gale conditions, especially with children. This is no place for bravado.

The former mining industry provides much interest and character, but also unique hazards. There will be mine shafts all around you, not all 'capped'. Keep well away, and keep dogs on leads. Where there is mine waste, the soil may be polluted. Wash hands before eating.

The maps provided in this book look very attractive but they are only sketch maps, so you may well want to carry the OS 1:25000 map.

The Cornish Countryside

Despite many pressures, Cornish farmers are still trying to make a living from the land you are passing through. Please respect crops, leave gates open or shut as you find them, and keep dogs under control when near sheep, especially in the lambing season.

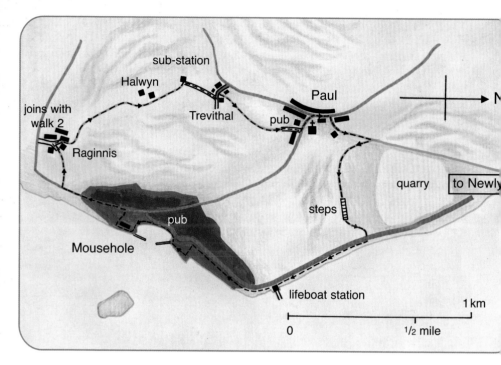

Walk 1   Paul and Mousehole

Distance: 5.3 km (3¹/₄ miles)   Time: 1¹/₂ hours
Character: An easy walk (except for stiles) with views over Mount's
Bay. Can equally well be started from Mousehole.

Park in Paul, an attractive village with a church (damaged by a Spanish raid in 1595) and a pleasant pub. Notice the monument to Dolly Pentreath in the churchyard wall, erected by Prince Lucien Bonaparte who was passionate about Cornish and other threatened languages.

From the Post Office at the village centre take the Penzance road, then take the first right down a lane signposted as a dead end.

Continue ahead on a footpath till you reach a stile. Cross it and immediately turn sharp right, almost back on your tracks. This path winds down past a well concealed quarry and (by steps) to the coast road – which has a footway alongside. Turn right along the road, passing the Pendeen lifeboat station, into Mousehole.

At the point where the road narrows and loses its footway, turn left down a narrow lane which leads to the harbour. Follow the streets and quays nearest the harbour, passing the Ship Inn (or perhaps checking out its interior!), then Keigwin House, the only building to survive the Spanish raid, and a further memorial to Dolly.

4

You will reach a car park by the far breakwater. Now walk on past the row of cottages which faces the sea, turn right at the end and then bear slightly right up a track which leads you to a T-junction. Turn left up the road. After 20m you will see a COASTAL FOOTPATH sign.

After 350m on the road, turn right up some steps to a stile. (One of the stiles on this section is defective and requires athleticism: you may prefer to go round by the road – see map.) A footpath leads across several small fields to the hamlet of Raginnis. Cross a stile on the left at the top of the last field which leads into the driveway of Raginnis House. Turn right onto the roadway, then right again to cross the front of 'Thatched Cottage' (see photograph above) and of its garden then turn left onto a wide grassy lane between outbuildings. Cut across the track ahead, cross a stile into a field and walk close by the left hedge. Keep by the hedge across a second field: at the end, turn right then shortly left through a gateway.

Further stiles lead you past the front of Halwyn farmhouse, then into a larger field. Keep the hedge on your left as far as an electricity sub-station, then take the track into Trevithal hamlet. Enter the hamlet by the metal gate at the end of the track, keep left, and in 40m turn right across a stile. Keep the hedge on your left across two fields, then cross the middle of the third, which brings you back to Paul church.

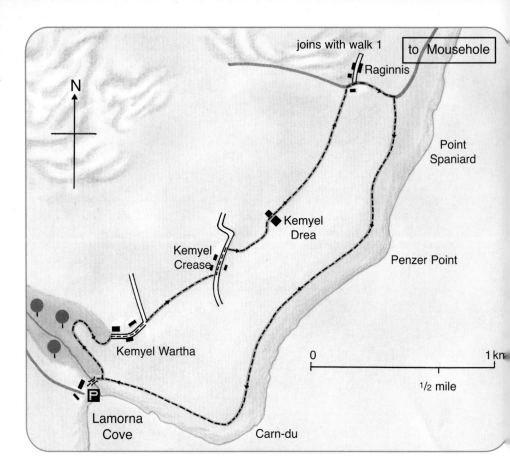

Walk 2   East from Lamorna

Distance: 6 km (3 1/2 miles)   Time: 2 hours
Character: A lovely walk, through farmland on the outward journey,
then back along the coast path with views of Mount's Bay and
Lamorna Cove itself. Many stiles: the last 2 km involves some quite
tricky clambering over boulders, as well as steps.

Park at the harbour car park (toilets, café, etc). Walk in front of the
row of cottages and cross the stream. At the fork bear left on the PUB-
LIC FOOTPATH which winds uphill through trees and past the disused
quarries.

   Turn right along the track through the hamlet of Kemyel Wartha,
then step over a stone stile onto PUBLIC FOOTPATH.

   Cross three fields (stiles and waymarks) to Kemyel Crease. Take the
track which leads onwards; 100 m beyond the hamlet turn right over

6

a stile. This path leads by way of a clapper bridge to a farm at Kemyel Drea. Here the path is taken between the yards over a series of stiles, gates and other obstacles (if the pallet is still there, the trick is to roll it clockwise).

Waymarks and stiles lead you on towards yet another hamlet, Raginnis: head for the gate to the left of the nearest house, and you'll find a stile into the lane. (You could at this point extend your walk by joining it with Walk 1.)

Turn right down the lane for 200 m, then, as the lane veers left, turn right onto the coast path. This starts by running level and wide for the first kilometre, but don't be deceived! The last stretch involves steps and scrambling over boulders and requires considerable care, but the views are well worth it.

When I last walked this way, on a late November day of alternating bright sunshine and squally showers, there was a magnificent rainbow right over St Michael's Mount, which more than made up for getting soaked.

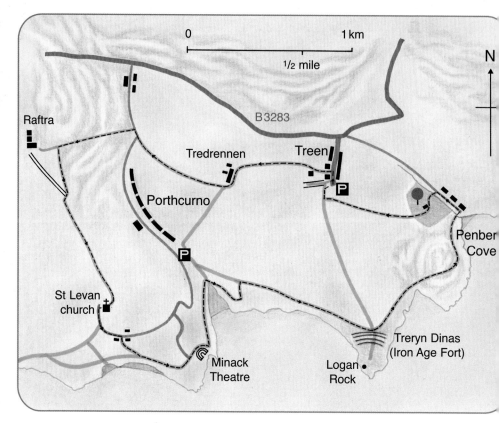

Walk 3   Treen and Porthcurno

*Distance: 7.4 km (4 1/2 miles)   Time: 2 1/2 hours – plus exploration time
Character: Initially windswept farmland, then stunning cliff scenery,
and finally a luxuriant sheltered valley: you will pass a church of great
character, the Minack theatre and Treryn Dinas, which is an Iron Age
fort (all of them well worth a visit) and an unspoilt fishing cove at
Penberth. Two vertiginous descents.*

Park in the village car park at Treen (SW395230) where there are public toilets, a post office/shop and a pub. Walk into the village and after
50 m turn left past Houses Farm, following PUBLIC FOOTPATH signs.
Cross six small fields to Tredrennen. Keep to the left of the settlement,
cross a wooden stile and turn sharp right, keeping the wall to your
right through the first field, then following yellow waymarks to a
road. Turn right along it.

After 100 m turn left (PUBLIC FOOTPATH) across three fields towards
silos, which are at Raftra. As you enter the fourth field (which contains

8

a large shed), turn 90° left across the field, to a waymarked stile, then another at the far right corner of a second field. Here there is a track, and two metal gates. Go through the gate on the right, and head towards the sea. This path leads to St Levan church which soon comes into view. Go through the churchyard and turn left along the lane, towards the sea, then uphill. Take the PUBLIC FOOTPATH to the right after the first house, which leads out to join the coast path.

At the Minack theatre, ignore the PUBLIC FOOTPATH sign leading up the drive: the coast path runs just to the left of the main theatre entrance, and spectacularly descends a precipitous flight of steps. (Vertigo sufferers may prefer to use the lane! See map.) Cross the back of Porthcurno beach and continue up and along the coast path. At a fork, the main path (blue waymark) just cuts off a corner.

As you reach the outer earthworks of Treryn Dinas, where there is a National Trust contribution box, a path to the left is a short cut back to Treen, then a path to the right heads for the 'castle' and a closer view of the famous Logan Rock. Take the middle path, which leads along the coast to the delightful fishing cove of Penberth.

Cross the stream and follow the lane inland for 300 m, then turn left on PUBLIC FOOTPATH. At a pair of cottages, turn left, then after 50 m turn right and follow the path uphill through a wood, then up across several fields (waymarked stiles and gates) back to the car park.

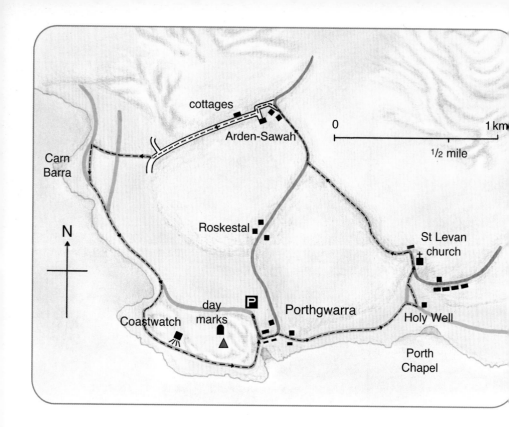

Walk 4 Porthgwarra

Distance: 6.8 km (4 miles)   Time: 2 hours
Character: Superb cliff scenery and pleasant farmland; the walk takes in both St Levan holy well and its delightful church.

Park in the car park at Porthgwarra (SW 371218) where there are toilets and a seasonal café. From the car park, turn left past the café, then turn right, COASTPATH MINACK. Follow the coastal path, marked by an acorn carved onto waymarks. Suddenly, St Levan's church will become visible: ignore the path which leads inland, but descend to the ruin of St Levan's well.

Turn left, inland, which will bring you to a lane. Turn left, pass the church, then turn left in front of 'Underhill' onto PUBLIC FOOTPATH. Cross a stile, keep the wall on your left, cross a second stile and keep the wall on your right.

After 50 m turn right over a third stile. Pass two gateways on the left. Cross a fourth stile, then follow the well-beaten path towards a farm on the near horizon. Turn right along a lane. Beyond the farmyard,

10

turn left (PUBLIC FOOTPATH) on the drive to 'Arden-Sawah'. Ignore the footpath to the right. Half-circle the farmyard, then turn right down a track, passing a pair of cottages.

Head towards the sea, keeping left at a junction of tracks, then after 50 m keeping right on a footpath. Cross another footpath (with a notice explaining it's not a public one). On reaching the coast path – unsigned but obvious because so heavily walked – turn left.

When it forks, take the path nearest the cliff, and after crossing a gulley keep to seaward of the Coastwatch lookout on Gwennap Head and of the two daymarks. Descend to Porthgwarra.

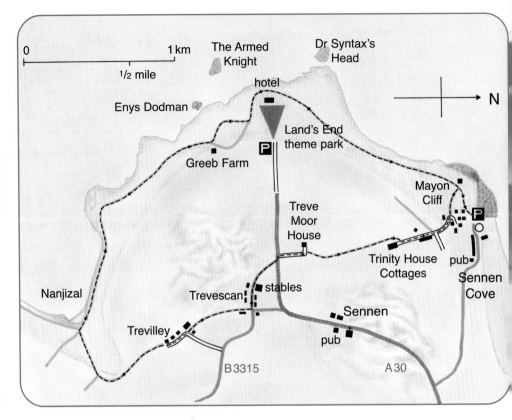

Walk 5   The Land's End and Nanjizal

Distance: 8.3km (5¹/₄ miles)   Time: 2¹/₂ hours
Character: Stunning coastline and a pleasant inland return. There are
two steep ascents, and round Nanjizal Bay the path goes very close to
the cliff edge, so take great care.

The walk passes through the Land's End theme park – which is 'pay-
as-you-go' so if you want to indulge yourself, feel free to do so! The
price of a day's parking at Land's End is little more than the car parks
in Sennen Cove, which may be full in high season, so you might want
to start from Land's End, which would also allow you to shorten the
walk if you wanted.

From the far end of the Sennen Cove harbour car park (SW 350263)
take COAST PATH LANDS END; climb the steps ahead of you and bear
right to the old Coastguard lookout, then follow one of the clifftop
paths – they diverge and merge again, and may be diverted to avoid
erosion. After 1.5km you will arrive at the Land's End theme park.

12

Continue past the front of the hotel and, by a choice of routes, on to Greeb Farm. After passing several coves you will come to the wide sweep of Nanjizal Bay.

Follow the path around the bay, where it goes very close to the cliff edge. Just above a tempting sandy beach, turn left inland and steeply uphill. As the route levels out, follow the path to a kissing gate and across three fields by a well-beaten path, to a gate. Take the track which skirts to the right of Trevilley. At a T-junction, go straight ahead (NO CYCLING) through the farmyard and into a (muddy) field. Keep the hedge on your right. Cross a stile 100 m beyond the wayside cross, then go through a small gate and across the front of cottages.

Turn left along the B 3315 – which might be busy in high season. On reaching the Land's End access road (a.k.a. the A 30) cross it and take the PUBLIC FOOTPATH down the track. At Treve Moor House continue ahead on the path, cross a brook and keep right up the slope (heading North, if you have a compass).

Follow a beaten path over several fields towards and across the frontage of a white-painted terrace (in a standard solid Trinity House design, which might look more appropriate if set in a Greenwich street than it does here). Join the lane and pass another terrace, then keep left downhill on a tarmac track. Take the lane that passes the entry-point of a dedicated cycle route. It soon curves to the left.

The track meanders to a sharp right turn. Go through the gate on the apex of the turn onto Mayon Cliff, and head for the coastguard lookout. Take the right hand fork here to get back to the harbour.

13

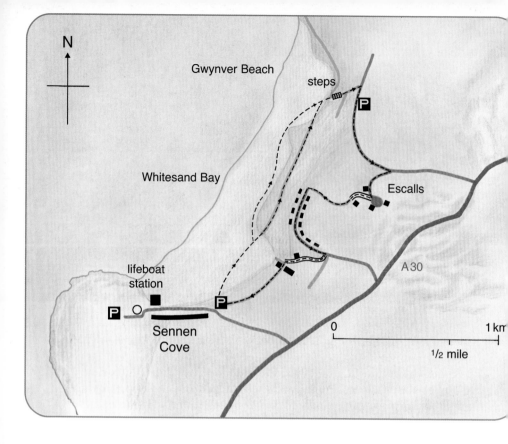

Walk 6 Sennen Cove and Escalls

Distance: 4.5km (3 miles)   Time: 1¹/₂ hours
This walk can easily be extended, or combined with Walk 5.
Character: Starts across the broad sands of Whitesand Bay, then an
interesting return through a countryside where agriculture is inexorably
losing out to the holiday industry.

From the Sennen Cove beach car park pass the café and head North
over the sands. At low tide you can go all the way to Gwynver Beach
along the sands, but at high tide you have to take a (slightly tricky)
path along the foot of the cliffs, which you pick up just below a poly-
gonal wooden beach cottage, guarded by its very own pillbox.

At the centre of the next sandy bay (Gwynver) take the steps which
lead up the cliff. (Alternatively, you might like to walk further along
the coast path, then return to this point.) As you climb the steps,
ignore the path to the right. Reaching a lane, turn right along it and
after 500 m turn sharp right.

14

Whitesand Bay, Cornwall's most westerly beach and one of its finest. This photograph was taken between Christmas and New Year, so there were only a few visitors to appreciate it with me. Cornwall in winter can be quite glorious for walkers

This will lead you, after another sharp turn, into the hamlet of Escalls which has a miniature version of a town square in front of Escalls Farmhouse. Turn sharp right down a track, which soon curves left past two 'renovated' buildings and becomes a grassy enclosed path.

At the end of the track, keep left onto a lane which serves a number of cottages and bungalows with magnificent views over the coastline.

Just before a red post-box, two PUBLIC FOOTPATHS lead off to the right. Take the one on the right (NO VEHICULAR ACCESS) which is a track leading down towards the beach. Don't worry about the exotic plantings, it really is a right-of-way for walkers.

You may of course be desperate to get back to the beach. If not, a path between the row of cottages (including 'Petra') and the cottage nearest the sea leads you by an inland route across the dunes and offers perhaps the best views of Whitesand Bay. It ends at the beach car park.

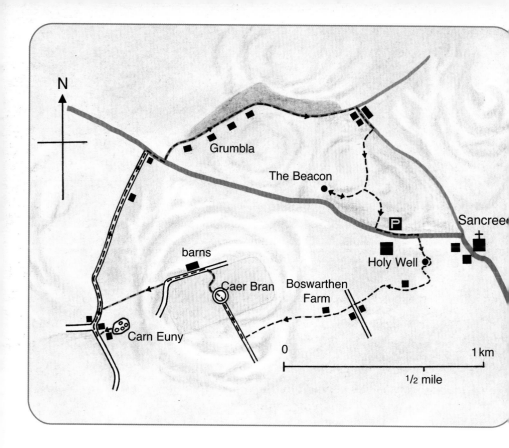

Walk 7　Sancreed Beacon and Carn Euny

Distance: 6.3 km (4 miles)　Time: 2 hours plus exploration time
Character: An inland walk mostly across farmland and open moor.
It takes in a holy well, an Iron Age fort and a wonderfully preserved
Iron Age village, including a fogou. Map and compass desirable.

Park in the long lay-by on the Sancreed to St Just road, about 500m
west of Sancreed church (SW416294). Walk downhill along the road
for 100m then turn right on a path to HOLY WELL. You will soon reach
the ruins of a tiny chapel, then the well itself which is decked out with
offerings.

　A path continues beyond the well, to the right beside the hedge. Go
down it for about 60m and you will find a stile on the right. Cross this
and head for a farmhouse, keeping a hedge on your left. Another stile
leads you round to the left of the farmhouse, then you bear right to
the next stile and cross another field. Reaching an old lane, turn left.
Pass a house and go up the path on the far side of a track.

16

Keep the hedge on your right across two fields, passing derelict Boswarthen Farm, then continue in the same direction (West then South-West) across four fields by stiles (not gates) which will bring you to a track. Turn right (noting the wayside cross).

Climb a rather muddy bridleway to Caer Bran hillfort, with a large main ditch and (on the north side only) an inner ditch. Within the fort the path branches; keep left. The path winds towards corrugated iron barns.

Turn left along the farm track, and after 150m continue ahead on a path. Reaching a track, turn left down to a group of houses, then take the PUBLIC FOOTPATH CARN EUNY.

After exploring this extraordinary site, retrace your steps and continue up the track, which will after 800m bring you to a road. Turn right and after 120m turn left (TREMETHICK CROSS) along a quiet lane. After 1km turn right at a junction (SANCREED). After a further 220m turn right through a gate – and take the warning notices seriously: Sancreed Beacon is riddled with ancient mine workings so stick to the paths. Follow a path along a line of telephone poles, then keep right and in time you'll reach the top of the Beacon (extensive views). You'll see some farm buildings about 300m away, which are just across the road from your car. Follow the main path down, then head in that direction.

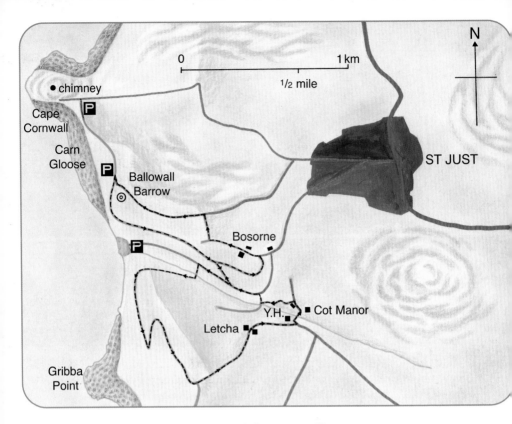

Walk 8 Carn Gloose and the Cot Valley

Distance: 5.7 km (3 1/2 miles)   Time: 1 3/4 hours
Character: A splendid walk, with varied cliff and inland scenery,
interesting remains of the mining industry and a magnificent ancient
monument. The footpath winds between cliff edge and dangerous mine
shafts, so children and dogs need to be kept under close control.

From St Just, take the Cape Cornwall road, then turn left on Carn
Gloose Road and park where the lane ends, at Carn Gloose itself
(SW354313) with views of Cape Cornwall to the north and The
Brisons rocks offshore.

   Head south along the coastpath (LAND'S END) passing many old
mine shafts. Descend to a junction of paths; carry on down and
inland ignoring side turnings. Reaching a tarmac lane, turn sharp
right (COAST PATH SENNEN). After 300 m turn left and cross the
stream. The path climbs to give a good view over Porth Nanven, then
turns sharp left and proceeds slowly up the cliff, passing a series of
clefts, which are evidence of early mining.

After 600m, the path starts to zigzag upward, before continuing along the cliff. Proceed along the cliff path to a point where it goes over a wall; leave it here, and keep left, inland. Cross a stile into a field. After 50m, keep left along a track. Entering a small field, keep left to a waymark at a gateway, where you bear right, diagonally across a small field and then to a cluster of cottages. Cross a stile and proceed down their access track.

Reaching the tarmac lane, turn sharp left, passing the Youth Hostel, down to Cot Manor. The lane peters out, becoming a footpath. As it does so, turn left along a PUBLIC FOOTPATH which winds through a jungle of buildings and gardens. Reaching a track, turn right, then left down the lane. After 200m keep right (COAST PATH CAPE CORNWALL) up the path by which you descended earlier.

After another 200m, turn sharp right. This tricky little path meanders uphill (mostly) to a stile, then steeply by further stiles to a tarmac lane. Turn left along the lane (not the 'Rosvean' track) between houses. The lane becomes a footpath. When it forks, bear right. After 250m turn left along a lane.

Some 100m beyond a lone chimney stack, just before you get back to your car, you will see on the left what you could be forgiven for thinking is another mineshaft, though larger than most. In reality it is Ballowall Barrow, a Neolithic entrance grave probably built around 4500 years ago. It was no mere pile of stones, but a complex structure, though altered in the Bronze Age and again by Victorian enthusiasts.

19

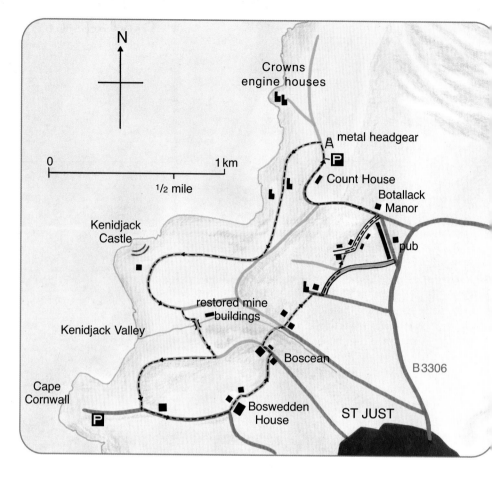

Walk 9   Botallack

Distance: 6.3 km (4 miles)   Time: 2 hours
Character: A wonderful combination of stunning cliff scenery and the remains of mines which functioned as recently as 1914. Relatively easy walking.

There is a large parking area at Botallack, near the metal headgear and just beyond the Count House (SW 365333). Turn right (North) and then left signed COASTPATH CAPE CORNWALL. You will get a good view of the famous Crowns engine houses, perched halfway down the cliff. They served a mineshaft which descended diagonally beneath the sea.

The path soon swings southwards. Bear right along the coastpath (yellow waymarks). After nearly 1 km, you will reach a headland on which lies an Iron Age promontory fort, Kenidjack Castle, which you

may want to explore. Cross a stile and descend to a track; turn left and after 150 m turn right down a path.

Follow the yellow coastpath waymarks to cross the Kenidjack valley; extensive mine buildings cover the valley floor. Turn right at a T junction and on reaching a track turn right towards Cape Cornwall. Unless you want to explore Cape Cornwall, turn left up the road, past a hotel.

When the tarmac road turns right at Boswedden House, you turn left through the hamlet and then right just before Lower Boswedden. Cross a stile and keep the hedge on your right through one field, and over a second stile. Now bear 45° left to a stile in the middle of the wall ahead of you. Continue over further stiles towards a white house with an engine house near it. Follow the waymarks to Boscean Farm. Emerging (from the top of a hedge!) onto a lane, turn left. Take a right fork down into the valley.

Reaching a lane, turn right and in 10 m left up a path. Follow a cart track uphill; then, between a farm and an engine house, continue forward over stiles along a clear footpath.

At the next engine house, turn right then immediately left along a track. When the track bears off right, go straight ahead over a stile (beside a flimsy metal field-gate) and between cottages. Join a track. At the road, turn sharp left back past Botallack Manor towards the mine.

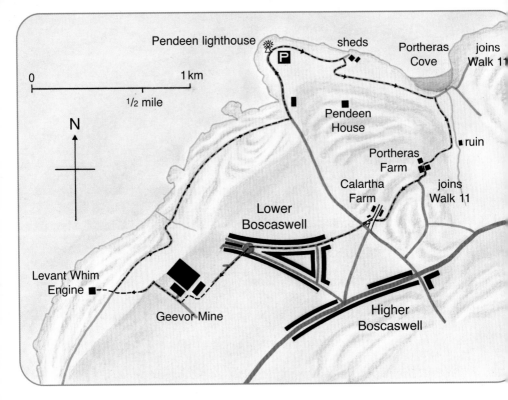

Pendeen lighthouse sheds Portheras Cove joins Walk 11

0 1 km

½ mile

N

P

Pendeen House

ruin

Portheras Farm

Calartha Farm joins Walk 11

Lower Boscaswell

Levant Whim Engine

Geevor Mine

Higher Boscaswell

Walk 10   Pendeen, Geevor and Levant

Distance: 6.6 km (4 miles)   Time: 2 hours
Character: Stunning coastline, a mining village and a haunting
landscape of post-industrial devastation. Geevor Mine and the restored
steam engine at Levant Whim are open to the public and both are well
worth visiting. This walk could be combined as a figure-of-eight with
Walk 11. Mining areas are hazardous: see page 3.

Park at Pendeen lighthouse (SW 380359) where there is further parking down the track if it is busy. From the lighthouse take the coastpath (ZENNOR). Bear left onto a track and follow it down to a group of fishermen's sheds. Just before these, the coast path turns uphill (waymarks) and zigzags to a gate. Continue along it to sandy Portheras Cove. Above the cove, follow the first waymark down, then after 100 m turn sharp right uphill at the next waymark post.

Climb steadily until opposite a granite ruin on the far bank. Take a right turn and climb steeply for 40 m, then bear left to a spidery metal gate from which an enclosed path leads to Portheras Farm. Turn left in the yard, and leave by the tarmac lane.

22

After 50m turn right over a stile, Keep the wall on your left for 100m; cross a stile on your left, then almost immediately one on your right. Now keep first the wall, then a farm, on your right. A small wooden gate ahead of you looks like an entry to a cottage garden: actually it's the footpath and leads you closely past a barn conversion to a track. Turn left along it, then after 20m fork right. Cross a minor road and head up a tarmac lane into the former mining village of Lower Boscaswell. Ignore all side turnings until you come to a broad space at the village centre.

Turn left towards the winding gear of Geevor Mine, now a museum. Keep left and follow the footpath into the overflow parking area. Head to the left of the mine complex. Follow the RECEPTION signs, pass the Mine Shop (which stocks many specialist books on Cornish mining), cross two wooden stiles and turn right down an enclosed path.

Turn left at a huge boulder, and follow a route which heads south and slowly approaches the coast. There are many paths through this strange and mournful landscape – a place of lost lives (fatal accidents were all too common) and now of lost livelihoods and devastated earth. Near the cliff edge you will find the restored headgear and whim engine-house of Levant mine, with a working steam engine. Like Geevor, the whim engine-house is open to the public and keeping alive the memory of Cornish engineers and miners. Now turn and follow the waymarked coast path back towards the lighthouse.

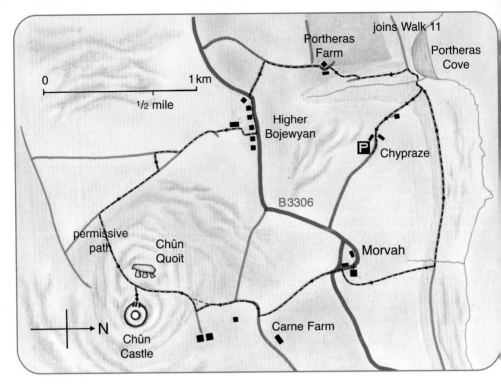

Walk 11   Morvah and Chûn

Distance: 8.2 km (5 miles)   Time: 2³/₄ hours
Character: A mixture of coast and moor, including Iron Age Chûn
Castle and 5000-year-old Chûn Quoit. Map and compass desirable

Park at Chypraze (SW 394355), where a field is used as a car park.
Turn left out of the car park, and at Chypraze House turn left through
a gate (blue waymark) down a track. Just before a modern cottage,
bear left down a path. When this joins the coast path, go forward
down towards Portheras Cove.

Cross a stream and climb, passing an emergency phone box. Bear
left at a junction heading inland up the side of a valley. At a junction
opposite a granite ruin, turn right. At the top of the slope, turn left
and after 100 m cross a stile beside a rusting gate. A narrow track leads
towards Portheras Farm. Join a tarmac lane for 500 m.

Just before the lane turns sharply right, cross a stile on the left.
Follow a beaten path, over further stiles to the B3306 road. Turn left
along it (beware traffic). After 200 m turn right at Bojewyan House.
Walk between farm buildings: the track bears right then left past a
bungalow.

24

Continue up a stony bridleway, later a track. At a fork in the track keep right, then after 50m turn left and after another 50m turn right in front of a gate. This track heads south, with an enclosed field to your left and scrub to your right. After about 500m, turn left across a stile onto a permissive path across a field, and then onwards in the same direction to Chûn Quoit.

Now bear right, and head for Chûn Castle, an Iron Age hill-fort, reused in the post-Roman period when it was a centre for the tin trade. Its massive double walls are nearly 90m in diameter, and once probably stood more than 5m tall (see photograph above).

Return to the Quoit and take the path which leads NNE towards the hamlet of Morvah by the coast. Follow the waymarks, which divert around a fragile ancient earthwork. When offered a choice of paths, turn left rather than going straight on. On reaching a track, turn left; at a crossroads, turn right down to a tarmac lane.

After 130m, at a bend in the lane, turn left over a stile. Follow the yellow waymarks. (In the first field, keep uphill to avoid its boggy centre.) You'll emerge on the main road. Go straight ahead, then keep right. Immediately before the church, turn right along PUBLIC FOOT-PATH around the churchyard and over a wooden stile towards the sea.

On reaching the coastpath, turn left. After 1km the path descends towards Portheras Cove, and turns inland. When it turns sharp right, you should turn left, retracing your steps up the valley to Chypraze.

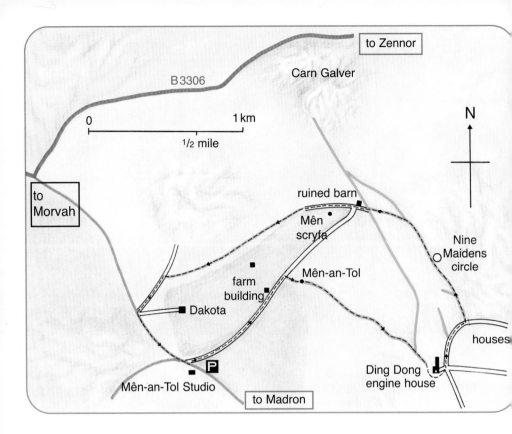

Walk 12   The Mên-an-Tol, Ding-Dong and the Nine Maidens

Distance: 5.8 km (3 1/2 miles)   Time: 1 3/4 hours
Character: A short and flat walk in beautiful moorland scenery, with
views of both coasts, two of Cornwall's most atmospheric ancient sites
and a disused mine. The terrain is open moorland with many
criss-crossing (and gorse-lined) tracks. Bare legs are inadvisable!
You will need a compass. Don't do the walk if it's foggy, as you're
likely to get lost without distant landmarks.

Park opposite the Mên-an-Tol Studio on the Madron-Morvah road
(SW 419344). Please don't obstruct any gates. Take the PUBLIC FOOT-
PATH TO MEN-AN-TOL. Walk up the track for 900 m, then turn right
where signed. The Mên-an-Tol is an arrangement of stones, probably
Bronze Age, of unknown purpose – but for many people its mysteri-
ous character makes it archetypal in this ancient landscape.

Now continue on the path which winds towards the engine house
on the near horizon – this is Dong Dong mine, which folk-lore said

26

was 'worked before the Flood'. Old mine areas are dangerous: my advice is always stick to the path and keep dogs on a lead.

About 50 m east of the engine house there is a junction of cart tracks. With your back to the engine house, turn left, initially heading North but soon swinging NNE towards a group of houses. Just before a metal gate, turn left up a path. Keep right when the path forks, to head NW. Soon Carn Galver – from this direction looking like a conical tor – comes in view. But first you come to the Boskednan stone circle, one of many called 'the Nine Maidens': in Cornish it is Dans Maen, stone dance.

Continue NW towards Carn Galver. After 300 m, at a fork keep left towards the ruins of a barn. Go through the gateway onto a track which after 100 m forks. Take the right fork. In the field on your left you will see a standing stone, the Mên Scryfa or 'written stone', which commemorates Riolabranus, or 'Royal Raven'. The writing apparently dates from the 6th century.

As you pass an abandoned farmhouse on the left, the path forks. Keep left alongside a stone wall with barbed wire on top. Continue heading West. (This path sometimes gets a bit overgrown with gorse.) You will eventually reach a farm track. Turn left along it to the road, where you turn left again back to your car, passing Dakota Farm.

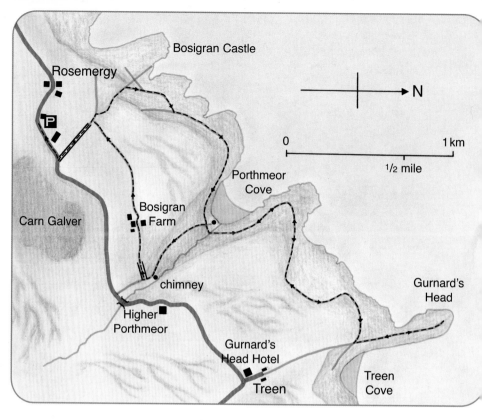

Walk 13   Carn Galver to Gurnard's Head

Distance: 8 km (5 miles)   Time: Allow 3 hours
Character: Mostly coast path (difficult walking in places), with a short inland return. Splendid views. Could be shortened to a circuit, but the there-and-back section is the best bit of the walk!

Park beside the twin engine houses of the old Carn Galver Mine (SW 421365) on the B3306 east of Morvah. Turn left out of the car park along the road, passing The Count House. After 200 m turn left down a track. Cross a stile into a field. After 50 m keep right, go through a gateway in the wall on your right, then turn left towards a rocky hillock silhouetted against the sea. This is Bosigran Castle, an Iron Age promontory settlement.

Go through a wooden gate. After 60 m when the path forks bear right, slightly downhill. When you reach the cliff path, turn right along it. It is quite rocky and uneven, and sometimes damp underfoot, as well as going near the cliff edge in places: keep dogs and children under control.

28

You will reach Porthmeor Cove, a deep inlet. Cross a brook. Turn left past a National Trust sign. Descend into the little gorge, cross the stream and climb steeply. It's then easier walking for 1.5 km. You will reach a crossing of paths. From the map you might be tempted to visit the Gurnard's Head Hotel and walk along the road back to Higher Porthmeor: I can recommend the pub (though I've never had time to test its ambitious menu) but the road at this point is not safe for walking.

The left turn takes you out onto Gurnard's Head, a narrow promontory stretching out to sea, with extensive views.

Now retrace your steps to the National Trust sign at Porthmeor Cove. A path leads up the valley.

Keep the stream on your left. Pass beside a chimney, then turn sharp right over a stile and along a walled track which leads up into Bosigran Farm.

To the right of the main house, a yellow waymark indicates the footpath, which then joins a track. The footpath continues in the same direction, parallel to the coast.

At first you follow the track. When it peters out at a gate, cross a gargantuan stile and continue with the field wall on your left over several fields. When you get near to the engine houses, turn left and retrace your steps up the track and along the road to your car.

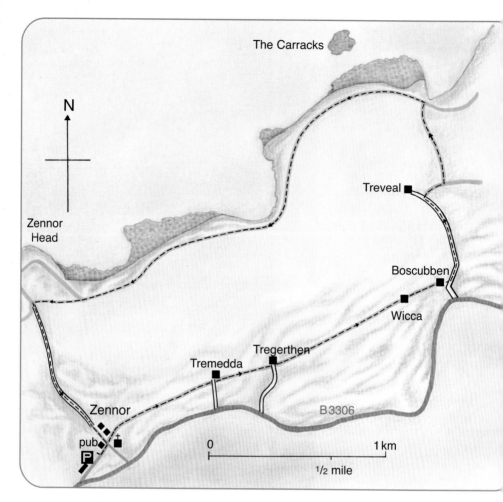

The Carracks

N

Zennor
Head

Treveal ■

Boscubben

Wicca ■

Tregerthen ■
Tremedda ■

Zennor

pub ● +■

P

B 3306

0   1 km

¹/₂ mile

Walk 14   Zennor

Distance: 6.7 km (4 ¹/₄ miles)   Time: 2 ¹/₂ hours
Character: Initially an easy and attractive inland walk, followed by
glorious cliff scenery. The coast path here is not particularly steep,
but it is very uneven, with granite boulders to scramble over in places –
quite hard going.

Park in Zennor churchtown (SW 454384). Walk up to the church,
keep left and then right, signed FIELD PATH ST IVES. Pass the graveyard
across a granite cattle grid. You will pass through a distinctive landscape of tiny fields separated by ancient granite cattle grids and walls
of massive stones. Cross farm tracks at Tremedda and at Tregerthen,
where the path can be very muddy after rain, probably due to a spring.

Walk through the farmyard at Wicca and continue in the same direction along a track to Boscubben, passing to the right of the house then bearing left down a track (TREVEAL – RESIDENTS' VEHICLES ONLY – FOOTPATH), ignoring a footpath on the right.

Continue down the track till you pass a house, then immediately turn right (RIVER COVE), down to a cattle grid. Here you turn left onto a path towards the coast and 'Seal Island'. This island is properly called The Carracks, but I have actually seen seals in its vicinity so it is not a boatman's myth!

Turn left along the coast path. It is far from easy walking in parts, so take care not to twist an ankle. After 2 km, a wooden waymark with a yellow arrow guides you right, to a fork in the path: take the upper path. (It is possible to take a lower path which goes round the next headland, Zennor Head.)

After climbing a slight hill you will reach a T junction of paths. That to the right is a well-walked path out to Zennor Head, but you turn left. After crossing a stile beyond the National Trust waymark for Zennor Head, this becomes a tarmac lane leading back to the church, the Tinners Arms (which is a consciously traditional pub and none the worse for that), a café, and the fascinating Wayside Museum.

This reprint 2008 First published 2005
Bossiney Books Ltd, Langore, Launceston, Cornwall PL15 8LD
www.bossineybooks.com

ISBN 978-1-899383-79-5

Acknowledgements
The maps are by Graham Hallowell
Cover based on a design by Heards Design Partnership
Printed by R Booth Ltd, Penryn, Cornwall